My *Secret* Weapon for Battling Mental Illness

CORI KELLY

ISBN 978-1-64468-319-4 (Paperback)
ISBN 978-1-64468-320-0 (Digital)

Covenant Books, Inc.
11661 Hwy 707
Murrells Inlet, SC 29576
www.covenantbooks.com

To all those who suffer silently with this
neglected and misunderstood disease.
May you find hope and validation here.

One day you will tell your story
of how you've overcome what you're going through now
and it will become part of someone else's survival guide.

CONTENTS

INTRODUCTION

LET ME BEGIN by saying that I am not an expert on mental illness by any stretch of the imagination. I have no degree or formal education that would qualify me to write a book such as this. I am, however, qualified to share my personal battle with this disease. It's my story, and I believe sharing it will help others who are plagued with mental illness. I believe the trials that God allows in our lives are meant to be used to encourage one another. In a sense, I want to pay my story forward to my fellow sufferers. I do this in the hope that they can take it and apply it to their own lives and reap the life-changing benefits.

I especially have a passion for all those who suffer in silence. I was watching a dance show on the TV one night, and one of the pro dancers in his practice session had a T-shirt on that said, "MENTAL HEALTH MATTERS." I was moved so deeply that I started to cry. I thought, *Are we finally starting to publicly take notice of this growing problem?* This gave me hope that maybe people will start to speak up. There are so many hurting people in the world that desperately need help. Up to two-thirds of all depression cases are undiagnosed. I find that number very disturbing. Why? I think it's because people mistakenly see mental illness as something they caused themselves or as a weakness thus preventing them from being open about it. We suffer in silence because we fear people's inability to fully comprehend what we're going through. We fear how we will appear to others and of their judgment. One of the most heartbreaking results of these stigmas is that they discourage people from coming forward and getting the help they need.

My battle with mental illness began thirty years ago. It actually arrived quite suddenly. I was about to begin my lifelong dream of starting a family. I couldn't have been more excited. God was good and blessed us right away. I had a wonderful pregnancy sans the awful heartburn. My first baby was born healthy with no problems pre or post-delivery. I felt great and was enjoying motherhood just as I expected. Things, however, weren't quite the same with my second baby who came on the scene just fifteen months later.

A few weeks after my second baby was born, I started feeling blue. I was sad all the time and not enjoying my role as a mommy anymore. I lost interest in just about everything. I cringed at the thought of all the responsibility that was now mine. I chalked it up to the baby blues and assumed that it would pass as soon as my hormones leveled off.

However, neither my hormones nor my blues did not level off and in fact were getting worse. I started having severe feelings of hopelessness as if I were in a dark tunnel with no way out. I felt overwhelmed with life and questioned my abilities as a mother. I could not stop crying as hard as I tried to pull it together. My husband would often come home from work to find his wife, an eighteen-month-old and a three-month-old, crying together on the living room floor.

The red flag went up for my husband after that and thankfully he took action. He made an appointment for me to see a doctor ASAP. The doctor diagnosed me with postpartum depression and suggested some medication, however, I wasn't convinced I needed any pharmaceutical help. As I fell deeper and deeper into the darkness, I knew I had to go back to the doctor. The second half of this story will come later.

The premise of this book is not just my story of mental illness. I also want to open your eyes to the concept of faith playing an integral part in the battle of mental illness. I am open and honest about my personal struggles in this book, which hopefully will attest to the fact that faith is the key to success in living with mental illness. I truly am living proof of that statement.

I am going to specifically outline how to let faith intertwine with your illness so you can live a more fulfilling life. My faith has saved my life on a number of occasions. I have been able to successfully navigate through my many years of chronic depression only by the grace of God. If it hadn't been for His divine intervention, I'm not sure you would be holding this book in your hands right now.

The most important thing I received from God during these times of suffering was hope. You can live without a lot of things in life but hope is not one of them. A person who feels hopeless is likely to give up on life as they can see nothing good in their future. They have no hope that their situation will ever change or get better. Friends, there is hope! The truth is that God is the only source of true hope. Psalm 62:5 says, "Find rest, O my soul, in God alone, my hope comes from Him."

God has taught me so much through my journey with mental illness. He has given me valuable insight and practical tools that I have put into practice. I call these my secret weapons. I want to share these insights and tools with you so that you may gain a fresh perspective and discover how faith can by your ally.

Even when you feel like you are all alone in your pain and suffering, I promise you, my friend, God is right there beside you. Even if you don't feel His presence or even acknowledge Him, He is still there. He will never leave you no matter what. God's love for us is unconditional. He longs to be a part of our lives and lead us to victory over our mental illness. 2 Chronicles 20:15 says, "For the battle is not yours but God's." Let Him go before you and guide you through your darkness. He is the only light you need!

If I've helped even one person, I will consider this book a success. Every life matters to God. The Bible says that He will leave the ninety-nine to go after the one. He desires that we are all given the right to live the abundant life regardless of the obstacles we face. You, my friend, are in His crosshairs, and He is drawing you to Him at this very moment. There can by joy and peace in mental illness but not through our own strength. He will enable you to persevere if you look to Him.

CHAPTER 1

Where's Dad?

IT WAS A typical October morning. I opened my eyes to the sun, streaming through my curtains with visions of breakfast dancing in my head. It seemed later than usual, and Mom hadn't come to wake me up yet, which was odd. As I lie there, I noticed something else that seemed strange. The house was eerily quiet. Usually, my older brothers were up and about, getting ready for school, and Mom could usually be heard in the kitchen clanging pots and pans around as she cooked us a hot breakfast. Her philosophy was that you learned much better with something hot in your belly versus cold cereal.

My six-year-old curiosity finally got the best of me, and I got out of bed to check out the situation. No one was on the second floor at all. No brothers, no mother, or father. Hmm…I decided to head downstairs, and as I approached the landing and rounded the bend. I peeked over the railing. I could see the TV was on, and black and white snow was all over the screen. Yes, there was a time when TVs actually went to sleep at night, and the four channels were replaced with snow. The living room lights were all on, which was never the case in the morning. I headed to the kitchen, and as I turned the corner, I found it was empty. No mom tending to my eggs or even a box of cereal on the counter. It was at this point that I started to worry.

Through tears that were now falling quickly down my cheeks, I looked out the kitchen window and noticed people in the backyard. This just added to my growing anxiety. I could see my brother, a policeman, and our next door neighbor standing around our garage. We had an unattached one-car garage that my dad always parked in because he had the nice car. As I opened the door to step out into the yard, my neighbor noticed and made a beeline over to me sweeping me back into the house. She was strangely nervous and elusive in her answers to my persistent questions. She was able to appease me long enough to get those eggs in my belly and find a nice dress for me to wear to school. She drove me to school and then took me into the office for a minute and whispered something into the Principle's ear. I would never know what that secret was for years to come.

It wasn't until many years later that I learned what really happened that day. I had been told by my family that my dad had a heart attack and died while getting out of his car. It wasn't until my late teens that my mother finally sat me down and told me the truth. My dad had taken his life in that garage by carbon monoxide poisoning. He had committed suicide, leaving behind a very distraught wife and three confused kids.

I didn't really know my dad since I was only six when he died. But from what I gather from family members, he had significant mental and addiction problems that were never admitted to or addressed. It seems it didn't stop with my dad either as my aunt (his sister) had made numerous visits to the hospital over the years for what was called back then a "nervous breakdown." It seemed as though there were some pretty deep roots on my father's side of the family with regard to mental illness.

My middle brother struggled really hard with my dad's death. He was at that tender age of eleven when boys really look up to their dads. Dad called him "Shorty" as he was always slightly challenged in the height department. They had a strong bond. So, it wasn't too much of a surprise that he took his daddy's death really hard. To compensate for his pain, he started experimenting with drugs and began what would become a downward spiral of addiction for the rest of his life. As he got older, the family picked up on some signs of bipolar as well. He would be soaring for days, sometimes weeks on end and then a switch flipped and he would be wallowing in the throes of depression. We knew that something was not right, and he needed to get some help. We tried many times to get him that help both as a teenager and an adult but without success. "I'm fine," was his pat answer, "don't worry about me."

His friends and family had many interventions with him. Again, the same answers were repeated, "I'm fine." Not a word we spoke was taken to heart, and he left these meetings usually with a six pack tucked neatly under his arm. My heart was so heavy, and I was deeply concerned that he might follow in his daddy's footsteps. But God gave me peace despite the circumstances. He reassured me that I (we) had done everything we could to help him. He was in God's hands now.

When the phone rings at 2:00 a.m., it's never good news. I was startled awake when I heard it and was even more surprised to find that I was talking to a police officer on the other end. He was asking me if I was related to the person in question. "Yes," I said, "he's my brother." The policeman then responded, "Well, ma'am, I hate to have to tell you this, but your brother was found dead tonight in a friend's garage. Apparently, it was carbon monoxide poisoning."

He was forty years old at the time. Dad was forty-one.

CHAPTER 2

The Key

IT IS IMPOSSIBLE to open a door using the wrong key. We are sure it's the right one, so we try every which way to get the stubborn thing in and turned the right way. Do we ever stop and think in this situation that maybe we're using the wrong key? Trying to fit the wrong key into the right hole is never going to work.

I was a latch key kid all through my elementary school years because my mom had to go to work after my father's death. I remember coming home one afternoon as a second grader and having trouble getting my key to work. I had no time to be fidgeting with the key as I had a restroom emergency on my hands. I was performing all kinds of acrobatic maneuvers, trying to keep the floodgates closed but after several unsuccessful tries with the door the inevitable happened. Now I had more problems than just a stubborn key to deal with.

My oldest brother fared pretty well after my father's death but my middle brother, not so much. He discovered how much fun it was to get in trouble and made it his life goal to be the poster boy for derelict youths. It was not an uncommon event in our house for the doorbell to ring at midnight with a policeman, standing at the door with my brother in tow. My mother was on a first name basis with the sergeant down at the precinct.

It got to the point where my mother had to get him out of the house for her sanity and my safety. After he moved out, she had all the locks changed. This was a great idea in theory, but she grossly underestimated the depths of my brother's passion for trouble. Locked doors or not he would always find a way to get back in. He even got around those chain link locks, which confounded my mother completely. He may have been a derelict but he was an ingenious locksmith.

These physical illustrations have a strong connection to our spiritual lives. In fact, these comparisons are really the premise of this book. This key is the first secret weapon I refer to on the cover. I have found in my life that Jesus is the key to living with mental illness. He is the key that unlocks the door of our minds, our hearts, and our souls. We all have a spiritual side as well as a physical side. I have discovered that I can battle mental illness much better with Jesus. He is the one, the only one, who can provide all that we need no matter what it is. He is our best line of defense and the most important weapon we can keep in our arsenal.

I was on a cruise recently and there was a very small pool in the spa area. When I say small, I mean about twice the size of a hot tub. They called it a "lap" pool, which made no sense to me at all since there was hardly enough room to float let alone swim a lap. After closer inspection, I discovered a huge jet stream, gushing in from one end of the pool. Then it hit me. The swimmer enters the pool, facing the gushing water and swims against the current. They were essentially doing laps in a stationary position.

I thought this is exactly what I feel like when I try and live with my disease without Jesus. You can try as hard as you can, but you won't go anywhere. You will be stuck right where you are facing an onslaught of opposition. You will strain to make progress, but the only result will be frustration and a total depletion of energy. Swimming against the current is never fruitful and a choice that will certainly take its toll on you physically.

God impressed upon me from the beginning that this was to be the key chapter of the book. Every other chapter will refer back to this main truth. The truth is that Jesus is and will always be the key to fulfillment and satisfaction in life. He is the only one—the only way—in which we can live a happy life. Don't get me wrong. When

I say happy, I don't mean life will be all sunshine and roses. That is one promise you will never find in the Bible. The word, "happy," in the Greek actually means blessed. And we are indeed blessed once we accept Jesus as the key for life here on earth as well as for eternity. Most of all, Jesus is the key that unlocks those pearly gates of heaven for every believer.

Friends, I am being completely honest when I tell you that I have tried fighting mental illness with Jesus and without, and I can tell you that Jesus is the only chance we have to win the war. He is the only way to victory. I was on my way to adding to the number of suicides in our family had it not been for my relationship with Jesus. He has been, and will continue to be, my only saving grace. He has been my shining light and only hope for survival. I can't even imagine fighting this battle without Him by my side.

One of Jesus's great attributes is that He is a true gentleman. He will never force you or coax you into anything you don't want to do. He gives each one of us a free will to choose and make decisions on our own. He will never break down the door of your heart to gain access. But He would love it if you threw out the welcome mat and invited Him in. Jesus truly wants to be a part of your life. Breaking and entering is not Jesus' style. He invites and the response is always left to us.

CHAPTER 3

Let's Roll

SEPTEMBER 11 WAS the greatest tragedy our country has ever seen. Four hijacked planes served as vehicles of mass destruction that day as they took aim to destroy the Twin Towers, the Pentagon, and the White House. Thankfully, through the bravery of some of the passengers on the flight headed for Pennsylvania Avenue, the terrorists' plans were thwarted, and the plane crashed in a little known rural town in eastern Pennsylvania.

One of the four planes hijacked that morning was Flight 93, which was initially headed to the West Coast, but after being hijacked, it turned around and headed for what authorities believe was the White House. The passengers on this flight knew it didn't look good for them because of the information they were getting from their mobile phones. Shortly after the hijackers took over the plane, they announced to the passengers that there was a bomb on board. I can't even imagine what I would be feeling after that announcement. I'm sure they prayed for a miracle that unfortunately never came. Some men, however, put their heads together and instead of focusing on the inevitable, they concentrated on what they could do to spare the country more tragedy. A few men had an idea, and they took it upon themselves to do something about the situation. Their plan was to attack the pilots and somehow recapture the plane. I would imagine they thought it was a long shot that they could somehow fly that plane to safety, but it didn't stop them from trying. They were heroes nonetheless.

One of the men, who sacrificed his life that day, was a man by the name of Todd Beamer. He was just an ordinary guy on a typical business trip. I'm sure he never imagined that he would become a hero that day. I'm sure he never gave one thought to the possibility of having to make a life or death decision. I'm sure he didn't have one inkling that he was soon going to have to make a decision that would affect him and his family for the rest of their lives. Yet all of this would soon become a reality. I'm sure he was tortured by the fact that he might not see his pregnant wife and two little boys again unless a miracle took place. Still, Todd chose to sacrifice his life. His widowed wife later wrote a book about her husband and his experience called, "Let's Roll." She named it that because those were Todd's last words the GTE switchboard operator heard before she lost all contact with the plane.

The title of that book has always stuck with me because of the words "Let's roll." Todd's "Let's roll" was the first lesson God impressed upon me in my battle with mental illness. Like Todd, I found myself in a situation that I had no control over. It was at this juncture in my life when God intervened and started to give me insights that would forever change how I dealt with my mental illness.

The first thing God showed me was there were two more words that He wanted to attach to the "Let's roll." He wanted it to say, "With me." Roll with me. He impressed upon me that the only way to roll was with Him. We can do nothing on our own. I can personally testify to that. All of my successes have come through the hand of God and not by my own efforts. I am very thankful that I don't have to roll alone. God is always right there beside me, cheering me on. I know I can get through anything as long as I rely on Him. I can honestly tell you that I only have the victory over my mental illness because of my rolling partner. I will "roll with Him" as long as I live.

CHAPTER 4

Words Matter

LIFE WITH MENTAL illness is a huge challenge to say the least. For the most part, people tend to view depression as an intentional state or something a person is responsible for causing. Nothing could be further from the truth. Telling someone to "get their act together," "just look on the bright side," or my personal favorite, "what in the world do you have to be depressed about" is mean and insensitive. These comments just add to the already existing hurt and shame. Never give advice or say things like, "You should or you shouldn't (fill in the blank). Sentences that start with "I" are always the best strategy. "I'm sorry you're going through this. I really want to be there for you. I would love to help you in any way I can."

There was a visibly depressed woman in my Bible Study group one morning. I had been concerned about her for a while when she came to class, looking so dejected. She came to class that day, and I could tell she was struggling even to be there. She didn't share much in group if anything at all. After class, I took her aside and chatted with her. She admitted to being depressed for a while. I asked her if she had had any suicidal thoughts. When she answered yes, I knew I had to take action. I grabbed another woman, and together, we made a plan. She would head back to our friend's house and intercept her kids when they got off the bus, and I would take her to the hospital. I thought she would argue with me about going to the hospital, but

I think she was actually relieved. I waited with her all afternoon until she saw a doctor.

When her husband got to the hospital, he displayed a very frustrated attitude. Rather than offer his wife love and support, he questioned her as to why she felt it necessary to go to the hospital. He offered neither a hug nor a kind word. It was almost as if he was angry at her for being there. You could see the pain and disappointment in my friend's eyes. I don't even think her husband realized how his words had hurt her. Words hold so much power and can either bring life or death to a person. She was dying inside in that waiting room that day from hurtful, careless words that obviously weren't spoken out of love. It was shortly after this event that my friend dropped out of Bible study. I'm sure she was embarrassed by her husband's response and lack of compassion. I never saw her again despite my efforts to contact her.

Do we ever take notice of the sad faces around us? The eyes are the window to the soul, and if someone looks hopeless, chances are that they're feeling the same way. It's easy to be drawn to happy people. It doesn't take much effort on our parts to interact with them. It's the hurting that we tend to ignore mostly because we are unsure of what to say. That can easily be dealt with using four little words. "I care about you." Yes, it may seem awkward, but you have no idea how those simple words can encourage someone who is dying inside. Don't ever walk away from someone who looks visibly distraught. Take them aside and interact with them. This will give you the opportunity to assess whether they are in trouble and need intervention. You could be saving a life by not walking away. You may be the angel God specifically sent to intervene on their behalf.

I do not believe that mental illness is being addressed enough or if at all in our schools. It hurts my heart to see it swept under the rug and not dealt with in our precious young people. Teachers, etc., need to do their homework and research the statistics, pertaining to the rise in suicide rates in preteens and young adults. How about replacing one elective course with a mental health class? It is my dream to be able to talk to young people in schools and encourage them to come forward and get the help they need. I want to reassure them that they are not "crazy" and they are simply suffering from a disease, which is, praise God, very treatable.

As I said earlier, words have the ability to kill one's spirit. I read once that it takes twenty positive comments to erase one hurtful one. We tend to hold onto that one ugly comment rather than replay any of the positive ones. The truth is that it's not possible to change how people speak to or treat us. But we do have choices about how to respond. The first thing we should do is to pray and enlist God's help. Ask Him to toss those hurtful words right out of your mind. Don't own them. Choose to reject the negative things that people say about you. The only opinion of you that matters is God's. And He happens to have a great opinion of you. You are his pride and joy, and He loves you more than you can fathom. Philippians 4:13 says, "I can do all things through Christ who gives me strength." This is one of my favorite verses that I use to encourage myself in difficult circumstances. It truly transforms my attitude and helps me to trust in God. Take those hurtful words to God and let Him heal your heart and protect your mind.

CHAPTER 5

Adjust

I GRADUATED FROM college as a Medical Transcriptionist. I'm sure some of you have no idea what that is or what they do. Well, in the dark ages, when I was starting my career and before there were computers and all the high tech gadgets we have now, doctors used Dictaphones to dictate their patient's charts. After seeing a patient, they would step out into the hallway and speak into this little walkie-talkie looking device that recorded their notes. Then the transcriptionist would take the tape and transcribe it on a good old-fashioned IBM typewriter (at least they were electric and if you were lucky they were equipped with white eraser tape). It was pretty easy except for when you got a tape from a doctor who didn't speak clear English and then it was an absolute nightmare. Start, stop, rewind. Stop, start, rewind. Thank goodness for improved technology.

I worked as a transcriptionist for a large group of doctors at one point in my career. I'll never forget this one particular doctor who had a clear case of OCD, which included adjusting all the pictures around the office. Every morning when he arrived, he canvased the entire office and straightened every pictures on every wall. Sometimes, he would just make the tiniest adjustment, but it had to be absolutely perfect for him to move on. I actually got a kick out of watching him make his rounds on all the artwork.

There is something in this illustration that I think relates to mental illness. The adjusting of those pictures is comparable to the adjustments we have to make in dealing with our illness. We go to Chiropractors to have our backs adjusted, we take our car into the shop to have our brakes adjusted, and who gets in the driver's seat without adjusting the seat and mirror? I got a new car a few years back, and there were so many different buttons to adjust the seat that it took me a good ten minutes to get it right. Up, down, front, back, tilt, straight. Thank goodness there was a memory button, so I didn't have to repeat the process every time.

This is another weapon that God gave me to fight my mental illness. He revealed to me the necessity of adjusting my life around my disease and firmly adhering to the restrictions it placed on me. I discovered very quickly that if I neglected to do this, I would definitely suffer the consequences.

The first thing we need to do is take a good look at our schedules and our activities. How full do we fill our plates? If we're already busy do we have to sign up to be the homeroom mom or help coach the Little League team? Is it wise to take charge of the bake sale when we're already feeling overloaded and stressed out? Will Gala night fail to be a success because we didn't help organize them? Believe me, all those things will get done even if you're not the one to do it. As one of my favorite (not!) employers used to remind me, no one is indispensable! Don't fool yourself by thinking that you are the only one who is capable.

I had four children under the age of seven before I was thirty. I learned my limitations very quickly as my depression was in full swing during these demanding years. I was never a homeroom mom. I never organized the Girl Scout cookie sale. I never went on field trips. I honestly signed up for very little because I already knew I had my hands full with four kids and a husband who worked twelve to fourteen hours a day. Yes, I did feel a tinge of disappointment for not being able to do these things, but I never experienced guilt. I learned early on that if I was ever going to survive this disease, I had to be selfish. Did you catch that? Let me repeat it. It's okay to be selfish! Our health and our families have to come first *before* outside commitments. Remember the old adage, "If momma ain't happy, ain't nobody happy." That is the absolute truth—at least in my house.

Putting our families first is not being selfish! If we don't take care of ourselves, our families will be the ones to suffer not the activities we didn't sign up for. I made no excuses when volunteers were asked for and my hand didn't go up.

I knew if I didn't protect myself from elective stress, I would be back in the doctor's office real quick. Those of us with mental illness have a choice as to how we take care of ourselves and the things we commit to. Nothing will overwhelm a depressed person faster than being overwhelmed. I learned early on that being too active would lead to a short slide into the dark pit. It's up to us to be honest and real about what we can and can't handle. We are the only ones responsible for our schedules. If you're not sure when to get involved in something or if you should let some things go, ask God for wisdom and direction. That's what He's there for. Give up the notion that we can do this life alone. I can't survive one day without my God, and truthfully I never want to try.

Looking back, I wish I had made one huge major adjustment in my life. I had an obsession with perfectionism when I was younger, and it was a great source of my stress and frustration as well as fed right into my depression. When I was raising my family, I put so many unnecessary expectations on myself. I was always overly concerned about having a spotless house, perfectly groomed children, and everything neat and in its place. None of my kids ever went to school with a wrinkled shirt or without every hair in place. Play-Doh was never allowed in the house! (Now it's a favorite activity with my grandkids). I never left the house without make-up even when I was just going to the gym. I never expected or allowed my kids to do anything around the house except make their bed. Their efforts didn't measure up to my standards, so it was just easier for me to do everything myself. Whatever I did, I had to be good at or I saw myself as a failure. In a nutshell, my life had to be absolutely perfect, and I was wearing myself out trying to keep it that way.

I am here to tell you that this is one of the most destructive ways you can live when you deal with mental illness. It's hard enough dealing with a full-time disease let alone being a perfectionist. I can't tell you how many meltdowns I had because I didn't get everything done around the house that I needed to. This was all the result of the pressure I put on myself.

One of the biggest bondages God ever freed me from was perfectionism. I don't remember when it happened or how it happened. I just know that one day being perfect didn't matter anymore. I started relaxing in my expectations and letting some things go around the house. I realized that I was not earning any extra points from God for having a clean tidy house. In fact, I began to think that I was actually wasting the precious time God had given me on insignificant activities. God surely was not going to care whether my windows sparkled or the laundry was always caught up. When I reach the pearly gates, one day, I do think He will look at what I did with my time here on earth. Did I use it to better myself or better the Kingdom of God?

I think that as my faith grew and my relationship with Jesus deepened, I became aware that I was living only for myself. It was all me all the time—my plans, my goals, and my agenda. I didn't seem to be involving God in any of it. He definitely wasn't my highest priority at the time. What I learned soon enough was that God should never be second fiddle to anything or anyone in our lives. We are setting ourselves up for a fall when we don't put Him first. When we don't adjust our lives around God, we are setting ourselves up for failure and an unhappy life.

CHAPTER 6

Bootstraps

WE'VE ALL HEARD the saying, "Pull yourself up by the bootstraps!" This phrase actually goes back to the nineteenth century when cowboys' boots had straps on each side of the boot and so they could grab them easily and pull them on. However, did you know that it is physically impossible to hold onto the bootstraps and hoist yourself up from the ground? Try it for yourself sometime. You actually have to let go of the straps to stand erect.

The original use of the word, "bootstrap," referred to a task that was considered far-fetched or impossible. It was used to describe something ridiculous. The current day meaning of the phrase refers to business. It means to start a business without any external help or capital. In other words, "I can do it by myself!" We do need to rely on something to stand up, but it has nothing to do with a bootstrap.

We were created by God to need a helper. We were never intended to be self-sufficient. What would be the need of God if we could do life on our own? In His infinite wisdom, He knew that thus we were made to rely on Him for everything. We have to put to rest the prideful notion that we are self-made successes and capable of living a satisfying life without Him.

As I was writing this chapter and thinking about bootstraps, I recalled a rather humorous experience from years past. My husband and I were on a weekend getaway when an incident happened that I will never forget. We decided to go horseback riding, an activity that we had only done a few times before. It was a beautiful autumn day with colorful foliage and perfect temperatures. I've always loved horses and thought of them as majestic creatures, but the one that came out of the stable with my name on it was seriously big. I didn't realize just how big until I got right up beside him. Even though I felt slightly (okay, a lot) intimidated, I was proud of myself for getting up on him on my first try.

Just as we were getting instructions on where our little tour was headed, another couple walked up to join the adventure. The husband was dressed in chinos and loafers, and the woman proudly wore a pair of daisy duke shorts and heels. I thought they obviously were at the wrong excursion location and not there for the equestrian event. However, the man spoke up and said that they were in fact there to ride horses. Now I like to be fashionable just as much as the next girl, but I felt my choice of jeans and tennis shoes was far more appropriate attire for this particular activity.

Mounting her steed proved a bit challenging for Daisy. She was having a hard time, getting those heels to cooperate with the stirrup. She was bound and determined that she was going to do this on her own, but it wasn't a pretty picture as she attempted and failed time and again to hoist herself up. Her Farrah Fawcet smile quickly faded, and now she was looking at the horse as if it were his fault. Her husband started getting nervous as he knew he would eventually take the blame.

However, this story doesn't end on such an entertaining note. Well at least for my husband and me. We were told to trot our horses a little faster down the path, so my hubby lightly kicked Freckles on the side, and off they went at lightning speed, dust kicking up all around. I could hardly catch sight of them as the horse continued his speedy departure like it was the Kentucky Derby. All was well until something spooked old Freckles, and he stopped on a dime tossing my husband head over heels to the ground. I could hear Daisy and Chinos giggling behind me, but it was nothing compared to my hysterical laughter. My husband picked himself and his 35mm camera up off the ground with a look of revenge like I've never seen. He was now chasing after Freckles, promising him he was going to reap the consequences of his bad behavior but old Freckles was long gone. I was still holding my sides laughing when I caught up to my dusty husband but soon realized there was something wrong. I wasn't the only one holding my sides.

We spent the rest of our romantic weekend nursing my husband's two broken ribs and bruised ego. We saw Daisy and Chinos later, sitting by the pool, drinks in hand, and resting comfortably after their equestrian adventure. Suddenly, they weren't so cute anymore after changing from their shorts and Chinos. We smiled and waved as we headed off to the hot tub for a good soak for those ribs.

While this story might be entertaining, it provides a great example of the point I'm trying to make with the bootstraps. Daisy's dilemma—mounting the horse—could have quickly been alleviated by one quick push from behind by her husband. Clearly, her husband telling her to "just grab on to the saddle, honey, and pull yourself up," was not working. All of his other helpful advice did nothing to alleviate her dilemma. Finally, the tour guide had enough, and he walked over to Daisy and gave her a solid push up on her steed. She quickly adjusted her shorts and heels and off we went.

This is exactly how it is with mental illness. Telling a depressed person to do something they can't is not only insensitive but does absolutely nothing to help the person. All of Chinos encouragement could not get his wife on that horse. She just wasn't able to do it on her own. The amount of shame and guilt that is heaped on a person for his "failure" to get up on their own and move on just adds to their existing pain and suffering. This example falls in line with a previous chapter as we see how the words others speak to us can be so degrading. Someone once gave me a great visual about words. They said, "Words are like shaving cream. Once they're out of the can you can't put them back." Hurtful words can't be taken back, and they are hard to forget. Sometimes (okay, a lot of sometimes), I struggle with using my words in the right context or saying them respectfully, so I have come to rely on a Scripture verse to help me. I pray it often especially in sticky situations. It's found in Psalm 141:3, and it says, "Set a guard over my mouth, Lord." Thinking before speaking is truly a priceless piece of advice.

CHAPTER 7

Numbers

EVERY TIME I research statistics on mental illness, I am completely blown away. The numbers and percentages are staggering, and they seem to get worse every year. According to the July 2019 issue of Time Magazine's special edition on Mental Health, it says, "Clinical depression affects 6.7% of U.S. adults or about 16 million people. The numbers are climbing significantly for children and teenagers. Among people ages 10–34, suicide is the second-leading cause of death. 14,000 young adults take their own lives in a single year." These numbers astound me, and yet they inspire me to do something about it. People need to be made aware of this disease, and there needs to be more research, more government funding, and more safe havens where help is available. We need to get serious about mental health in this country!

Time Magazine also gives some reasons for this growing trend. Their research points to social media and the loss of oral communication. This didn't surprise me as I watch it happening all around me. Personal interaction is being replaced with phones, Facebook, Instagram, etc. Time states that "technology may play a part in young people's feelings of being alone or cut off. One recent study from the University of Pittsburgh found that people ages 19–32 who spent two hours or more a day on social media were twice as likely to feel isolated as those who spent less time. Loneliness can be tied to higher rates of depression, anxiety, and self-harm among young adults." I recently walked into a meeting room at our church and found four teenagers, sitting altogether at a table, each holding cell phones in front of their faces. Not a word was being spoken among them. It made me so sad. Unfortunately, this is the world we now live in. I believe our suicide rates will continue to grow as we stay plugged into devices and unplugged from the world.

We were not created to live without face to face relationships. God intended us to live as social beings. God said in Genesis 2:18, "It is not good for man to be alone." God knew Adam would need a partner, a companion, and someone to share his life with. Thus He created Eve. We were never intended to live life alone without human interaction. Nowadays, the only interaction happening between people is taking place via text, Twitter, e-mail, or Facebook. This generation of young people have hundreds of friends on their Facebooks, but how many can they count on in a crisis? That goes for adults too. Spending time with friends is so important, and it is how we were wired. Everyone needs that friend or two that they can call in the middle of the night if an emergency pops up.

The National Institute of Mental Health (NIMIH) states that their data shows that half of all mentally ill people fail to seek treatment because of the stigma that is still attached to it and the limited access to help. Our homeless population is full of people who are mentally ill, but the resources just aren't there to help them. It breaks my heart. And it makes me wonder if there will ever be a place for these people to go. Their numbers will only continue to increase with this growing epidemic of mental illness and no intervention available.

Recently, I was at the doctor for my annual checkup. After I was finished, the nurse came in and asked me to do a series of simple tasks. One was to walk down a short hallway and back in a straight line. Another one was to draw a picture of a clock and then make it read a certain time. The final assessment was an extensive questionnaire screening for depression. "What is all this for?" I asked the nurse. She informed me it was required for all Medicare patients to screen for dementia and mental illness. What a novel idea!.

I think depression screening should be mandatory in all doctor's offices no matter the age or specialty. I don't mean just checking off a box on a form. I'm talking about an in-depth questionnaire that would be assessed and discussed with the doctor. I've checked the depression box on every doctor questionnaire I'm asked to fill out, and not once have I had a physician follow up on that checked box. Not even after giving them my list of meds do they ask how I'm feeling. Why is this? I don't think doctors treat the whole person anymore. I think they believe they are only responsible for the "chief complaint" written on the form. Mental health screening in every doctor's office has the potential to identify those who need to seek treatment. Yes, this might take up a few extra minutes of a doctor's time but wouldn't possibly saving a life be worth it.

I can't close this chapter before taking a moment to say something to all parents with children. If you even remotely suspect your child may be depressed, get him or her to a doctor as soon as possible. If you're not happy with what the first doctor said, get a second opinion. Trust what your paternal instincts are telling you. I didn't get to practice this soon enough with my sixteen-year-old son. I took him to the doctor for an evaluation because I suspected he was depressed. I was told, "It's just normal teenage stuff." I wasn't totally convinced given our family history. I never got the chance to follow up with a second opinion as my son tried to take his life soon after his initial evaluation. Obviously. he was struggling with more than "normal teenage stuff."

Trust your gut. If the diagnosis doesn't sit well with you, don't stop there especially if you have a family history of mental illness. I watched my four children very carefully growing up. I didn't waste any time taking one or the other for help if I saw any signs that something was amiss. If you are waffling on whether to take your child to be evaluated, do it. Better to be on the safe side than deal with any "if onlys" down the road.

CHAPTER 8

Miracle Meds

GOD CREATED ALL things for good, and I believe medication is one of them. He wouldn't have given researchers the ability to come up with these drugs if they weren't meant to be used to help people. Medication to treat diabetes or hypertension is no different than medication needed to treat mental illness. Sure, the scientific components vary, but the end results are all the same. They treat the disease effectively. This is exactly what I tell people who challenge me on the medication issue. Somehow, they think that mental illness doesn't fall into the disease category, but the "you should be able to kick this on your own" category. Try telling that to a diabetic!

My introduction to medication came when I was just twenty-five. As I mentioned earlier, a few weeks after the birth of my second baby, I was suffering with a pretty bad case of postpartum depression. What surprised me though was that I had no trouble with my first baby born fifteen months earlier, so this threw me for a real loop.

My husband insisted I see a doctor, and he did officially diagnose me with postpartum depression. He wanted to put me on medication, but I was adamant that I could deal with it by myself. I remember thinking that God and I would work it out together. Aren't we supposed to rely on God for everything I asked myself? I was putting my faith into action. I could do this! However, I discovered rather quickly that *I couldn't do it on my own*. After more time passed with no improvement, I had no choice but to trust that God was in control, and I had to try the medication. I was told it could take up to six weeks to feel the effect, but by the third day, I was already feeling better, and within a month, I was back to my old self again.

God gave me great insight into the debate over faith vs. medication from this experience. There are those who preach that if your faith is strong enough, it will cure everything, and we shouldn't have to rely on medication. What God impressed upon me is that my faith did play a part. I prayed to God for help, and He came to my rescue *through* the provision of the medication. God allowed healing to take place not by some grand miracle but as a result of God's giving man the ability and the resources to create the drugs. God provided a way for me to live an abundant life through the divine intervention of pharmaceuticals.

Medication can indeed be used as a weapon to fight mental illness. If it weren't for God, we wouldn't have any access to this weapon, which to me is a scary thought. I thank God that He has provided for me in this way. There is an old Steven Curtis Chapman song titled, "God is God." One of the lines in the song has always stuck with me because it sums up my absolute need of God in my life. The line is, "Can I even take a breath without God giving it to me."

CHAPTER 9

Poop Out

BELIEVE IT OR not, the term, "poop out," is a real psychiatric term. Psychiatrists use it when medication stops working for no apparent reason. Sometimes, being on a medication for a number of years can reduce the efficacy of the drug, so it just stops working (poops out). I became very familiar with this mystery of pharmacological science a number of times over my many years of depression. I also realized that medications don't have to stop working to throw you into a full-blown depressive episode. Stressful circumstances can also cause medications to stop working like they should.

I have lots of stories I could use for illustration here, but this one is hands down one of the worst poop outs I've ever experienced. I was humming along pretty well until my husband, and I decided we needed a new kitchen. Our house was over twenty years old and was way overdo for a facelift. However, when we decided to go ahead with the project, we neglected to consider our eighteen-month-old grandbaby that we were babysitting full time. That in itself was a challenge. She was an extremely active child and possessed one of the strongest wills I've ever encountered. Believe me when I tell you that I was the one who couldn't wait for naptime.

However, I was feeling pretty stable at the time and thought I could handle the mess and inconvenience regardless of our sweet bundle of joy. I should have known better because I knew I didn't do well when I was overloaded. Juggling contractors, a baby, and a torn-up kitchen overwhelmed me pretty quick. When we had to move the refrigerator and half the kitchen into our family room, it almost toppled my apple cart. It was then that I began to think I grossly underestimated this project.

One day, in the midst of all this chaos, I accidentally let a Pamper slip into the washer with the other laundry. When I opened the washer forty-five minutes later, I almost started to hyperventilate. There were thousands of teeny tiny little balls of some kind of a sticky jelly-like substance stuck to every inch of clothing as well as the whole inside of my washing machine. I was already crying before I pulled the first piece of clothing out. This wasn't the last straw, however, that broke the already precarious camel's back but it was right around the corner.

Besides the explosive diaper in my washer, the other catastrophic event (to me) involved grout. I walked into the house one afternoon and found that the tilers had used the wrong color grout on the kitchen floor. Of course, I immediately lost my mind. For some reason, the only thing I could thing to do was to call my sister-in-love to vent. (I did this a lot. The woman is a saint). Unfortunately, for him, her husband picked up the phone.

He didn't even get the word hello out of his mouth when I started sobbing. I was crying so hard he could barely understand who it was or what they wanted. After a long drawn out barely intelligible conversation, he was finally able to pick up on the problem and went on to explain that the grout would dry to the right color and not to worry, which is exactly what happened. As you might expect, this renovation brought on a full-fledged medication poop out. I went in to see the doctor as soon as I could and got started on a new regiment of drugs, which thankfully kicked in very quickly. I have since ruled out all house renovations. I will move before I redo one more room.

If you're on medication, and it just doesn't seem to be working anymore or you just feel like something is off, don't hesitate to schedule a visit with your doctor. The longer you sit and wait, hoping things will work themselves out, the harder it will be for you to bounce back. There are some medications I have been on for over 10 years, so I keep in tune with any changes in my mood. Being responsible and staying on top of any potential red flags is all part of proactive mental illness treatment. Like all diseases, it's always better to be on the offense than the defense. Attacking the problem is much easier than having to defend against it later. Because I've been in the pit so many times I do everything in my power to avoid visiting it again. I know I should be concerned when I begin to cry over nothing and can't stop. It's always my telltale sign that something is going awry. When pulling myself together is an impossible feat, it's time to make that phone call.

Moving on with life when the pit has sucked you in requires a lot of prayer and perseverance. The first thing I do is pray, and pray some more. Jesus is always my go-to first. Then I pick up one of the weapons I talked about previously and just begin to "roll with it." I can't control my emotions, so why try? If I cry, I cry. If I want to sleep, I sleep. If I need to miss a prior commitment, I bow out. If I need help, I ask for it. I know I can't do it alone.

I've been in countless social situations while in the throes of a depressive episode where I end up in a puddle of tears. However, I have found some good things that have come out of it. As is always the case, God takes whatever pain I'm going through and uses it to benefit someone else. So, I have gotten pretty comfortable crying in front of people. What I've discovered is that people are very sympathetic to whatever you're going through and show great compassion. I've also found that crying can be a bonding experience. It opens the door for deep conversation instead of the usual, "What's new?" or "Great weather we're having."

I can't tell you how many times I've randomly mentioned my depression in a group setting and everyone starts sitting up and paying attention. Fellow sufferers are more than willing to share their experiences after I've spoken us. I have seen first-hand from speaking to various groups the extensive number of people who are personally suffering or have a friend or family member who is struggling. It saddens me that there are not more opportunities for the mentally ill to come together as one to share and encourage one another. I ask myself what I can do to help people fight like God has taught me. I'm hoping that by writing this book, it will touch people and encourage them to pick up this secret weapon and give the battle over to Him.

CHAPTER 10

But God…

NO ONE ON the face of this earth is immune to pain and suffering. No one. Even if some people seem to have it altogether, they don't. Most people would like you to believe that their lives are perfect and all is well in their world. I do not believe that. In fact, I am suspicious of people who give off that persona. I say this because my Bible says otherwise. John 16:33 says that "in this world you will have trouble." Not you *might* have trouble, but you *will* have trouble.

We all must succumb to trials whether we like it or not. Some will seek comfort in family members, friends, or even drugs or alcohol. I can tell you from experience that none of these things will help or offer you the comfort that your soul cries out for. The only hope we have when life throws us a curve ball is faith. Only faith in Jesus can supply everything we need to get through the challenges that come our way. Depending on anything or anyone other than Jesus will be a futile effort. We were created to rely on one person and one person only. The Bible also talks about Jesus being an anchor for us in Hebrews 6:19, it says, "We have this hope as an anchor for the soul, firm and secure." The main reason a ship needs an anchor is to ride out storms, so that it is not blown off course or dashed into the rocks or reefs. Even in a safe harbor, a ship needs an anchor, so that it will not drift or sink. We all need an anchor for our souls so that we do not destroy our lives. This is a great analogy of what Jesus does for us in our storms.

Jesus and the disciples were out on the water one day when a horrendous storm blew in. Jesus was asleep in a comfy corner of the boat catching up on some much-needed rest. The waves started crashing over the side of the boat, and the disciples feared the boat might capsize and they were going to drown. They panicked and woke Jesus and probably, I imagine, with a little attitude in their voices said something like, "Hey Jesus what's up? Aren't you going to get up and save us before we die?" Jesus then stood, spoke to the wind and rain, and said, "Quiet. Be still." Immediately, the waves calmed, and the seas flattened out. The disciples stood there with their mouths, hanging open, thinking who was this man who could command even Mother Nature?

If Jesus could make even Mother Nature obey Him, what makes us think He couldn't do wondrous things like that in our lives? The Apostle Paul talks about "faith that can move mountains" (1 Cor. 13:2). Faith in Jesus can calm our storms and move our mountains just as easily. There is one prerequisite however. We must follow the example of the disciples and call out to Him first. They didn't concoct some elaborate or lengthy prayer they simply cried out, "Lord, save us," and Jesus took action. If you feel like you're drowning and have no one to hold onto, cry out to Jesus. He stands ready and willing at any moment to come to your aid. To be your anchor in the storm. It doesn't matter the situation or circumstance. Nothing is too big or too hard for God. I experienced this firsthand when my sixteen-year-old son didn't come home from work one night and was missing for three excruciatingly long days.

When my son got his driver's license, I was ecstatic. Most parents will tell you the opposite, but I was thrilled not to have to drive him around everywhere especially when I was taxiing three other children every day. Unfortunately, car keys to a really cool car didn't appear alongside his birthday cake, so he was stuck, driving the family minivan, which of course he was absolutely thrilled about. So, back and forth to work he drove in our sporty Town and Country. I often had to remind him that it was still better than mom dropping him off at the front door. Score one for mom.

One August night, right before the start of the new school year, my son didn't come home from work. At first, we didn't think much of it because he was a super responsible kid, and sometimes, he stayed late to help clean up. After about an hour of waiting, my husband decided to take a drive to his place of employment. He wasn't there. He was told he left at the usual time. So then, he tried different routes, thinking he might have taken a short cut. There was no sign of him or the van anywhere. After my husband got home, we called all his friends to see if they had seen him. No one had. Finally at midnight, we were beside ourselves, so we called the local police. The officer said there was nothing he could do until morning. This was extremely unsettling, but there was nothing we could do. Except pray. And pray we did. As soon as the officer left, I grabbed my Bible and headed for my bedroom. I opened it to the Psalms because I have always found great comfort in this particular book of the Bible. Our first miracle happened that night when by the grace of God, I was able to get any sleep and even more impressive was the fact that I rested peacefully.

The next morning, the local police arrived along with a few FBI agents. They told us that they had found the van parked in a parking lot about ten miles away. They were surprised to find his work hat, wallet, and car keys all neatly placed beside the driver's seat. Surrounding the area was nothing but woods, some commercial buildings, and a bridge spanning a ravine. Nothing remarkable. The car was dusted for fingerprints, but there were none other than my son's. We continued to pray and trust God that our son would be found. I couldn't believe the sense of peace I experienced even in the midst of such a horrifying ordeal. It was obvious that God was right there encouraging and comforting us.

The nightmare continued for two more days. We still had no clues and nothing to go on. Friends and neighbors came bringing food and taking the other children to their houses. By this time, his disappearance had hit the news, and a local TV station showed up on our doorstep. I couldn't face them, but my husband calmly stood before the camera with a microphone in his face and proclaimed that he was certain our son would be found because our faith in God was going to bring him home.

The police were trying hard to remain positive, but they were honest with us and told us that the odds of a child being found alive after twenty-four hours were slim. This didn't faze us because we knew our God was bigger than statistics. We kept our prayer vigil with our friends from church and our neighbors. We were anchored in our faith and rested in the arms of Jesus.

On the morning of the third day, the police chief called and said he had a "hunch" about where to look for our son. He told us he was going to send a police helicopter and team of officers with rescue dogs to the wooded area across from where my van was found. We sat and painfully waited for the phone to ring. When it finally did, the whole house seemed to jump up as my husband made a beeline for the phone. The words we so longed to hear for three grueling days were spoken, "We have your son." He was not in the woods, but in the ravine under the bridge. Our son was alive but in serious condition. The chief told us Life Flight was on the way as we all collapsed in each other's arms in a chorus of "Thank you, Jesus." My husband, daughter, and I flew into the car, took off like a flash, and actually beat Life Flight to the hospital. It was the scariest car ride of my life.

When we arrived in the trauma unit, they took us back to see him. I was chomping at the bit to see that our son was okay. I also couldn't wait to ask him what happened. How did he get in that ravine? The first thing I did was kiss his dirty face and then I asked the question. My son then shocked everyone in the room by saying, "I jumped. I jumped off the bridge over the ravine." My son had tried to take his life by leaping off a bridge. He fell five stories and laid there for three days in and out of consciousness. When he was lucid, he told us he did cry out for help, but he was too far removed from traffic. But God knew right where he was and led the police directly to him!

Don't ever think anything is impossible with God (Matt. 10:27). Don't ever think your problem or your situation is too far gone for Him. Our God is a big God, and He can handle anything we throw at Him. As this story about my son so perfectly illustrates, God is still in the miracle working business. We were the recipients of one of the greatest miracles we had ever been handed. Our faith and trust in God saw us successfully through the most traumatizing experience we ever could have imagined. It was only by the mercy and grace of God that our son was kept from the jaws of death and given back to us. The suspicion the police chief had that morning was not a coincidence. There are no such things as coincidences when it comes to God.

Our son had a plan to end his life but God had a different one. We think we're in control of our lives but God ordains our every step. He has a purpose for each one of us, and we can't stop it. His will, not ours, will prevail. He is the only One who knows what's best for us. Oh, we think we know. But we aren't able to see the whole picture like God. He is the only one who can see into the future.

So, why didn't the doctor, my son, saw two months before his attempt see any signs of depression? Believe me, I've asked myself that question many times. The only answer I can come up with is that some people with mental illness are master manipulators. They know how to play the game and what answers the doctors want to hear. They are very good at hiding their true feelings and are able to portray a seemingly happy well-adjusted person. In short, they play the system because they don't want to deal with the problem or they refuse to admit that there is anything wrong. It's hard to admit you are struggling mentally so we try and keep it under wraps. There are many people with mental illness who live like this. Fear trumps their acknowledgment of the problem, so they push through life as best they can.

How can we change this growing problem? How do we encourage people who are suffering to come forward and get the help they need? Believe me, as a mental health advocate, I ask myself these questions over and over. What can I do to bring attention to this disease? How can I make a difference? The only answer I can come up with is simply to talk about it. Put it out there to encourage others to come forward. Social media is a perfect venue for talking about things like this. You would be amazed at how many people comment on anything I say concerning mental illness. There are so many people out there, thinking they are all alone in their pain, and no one can possibly understand what they're going through.

I used to write down in a small booklet of faith all the places in town that offered free clinical help and shelter and hand them out to the homeless on street corners. I would put $5 in it, so they wouldn't just pitch it but discover the info I had written down inside. Part of the problem is that people don't know where to go to get help. That's why it's so important to share these resources and information.

CHAPTER 11

Bits and Pieces

I HAD A Bible study teacher years ago use a vivid word picture to describe how God weaves our lives together like a perfect tapestry. She talked about how our lives are works of art that God sews together to create a beautiful masterpiece. His masterpiece. Each vibrant colored thread, representing a different aspect of our lives. She told us God's masterpieces were like snowflakes, no two were alike. She helped me understand that what I perceived as dysfunction in my life was actually God working on my tapestry. Joining together little pieces of cloth to make a complete representation of me. Of my life. Think about it.

When you look at a tapestry from the finished side, what do you see? You see a beautiful wall-hanging, an exquisite work of art. Its beauty fascinates you as you look at how perfectly every thread is sewn. But if you look at that same tapestry from the back, all you will see is a jumbled mess of threads and knots. This is how we see our lives. Far from what God is seeing on the other side.

God takes our lives, pain and all, and creates a one of a kind portrait of beauty. He takes what we thought was a complete mess and forms it into a priceless treasure. Our inclination is to only see the jumbled mess of threads on the back of the tapestry and forget the other side. We forget that He is always working away on us to bring His plan to fruition. We can't see how it all fits together, but He can. Our tapestries will one day hang in our rooms in heaven. A wonderful reminder of how God used every experience in our lives for good and to create a thing of beauty and perfection.

Think of your life as a parade. God sees the whole parade from beginning to end all in one glimpse while we sit on the curb watching it go by float by float, marching band by marching band. We see only small snippets at a time. We know there is an end, but it's not in sight yet, and if it's a Disney parade, we might not see the end for days. God sees what we can't. He sees how and when our lives will come to a close and everything that happens until that time. It's all been in the works since the beginning of our lives. He had it all planned from the beginning of time, and His plan was put into effect the moment we took our first breath. Everything that happens to us from that point on is no surprise to God. He knew when our trials would come and what their purpose would be.

All things have a purpose. There is a reason we are suffering with mental illness. We don't understand it, but God does, and He sees the good that will come of it. We may not understand it, but that's where faith comes in. God is looking to see how we will weather our storms and if we will trust Him. Are you willing to put your faith in God? He promises in His Word that He will turn our suffering into rejoicing. I have already experienced this as I walk through my illness day by day. King Solomon, the wisest king in the Bible, tells us in the book of Ecclesiastes, "There is a time for everything and a season for every activity under heaven." He is saying that there is a season and a reason for everything that happens to us in our lives. The question is how we will respond to these seasons. Will we react in anger and bitterness or will we have an attitude of acceptance and belief that God is in control. Always.

We can't lean on our own understanding and try to analyze why God does what He does. He is God, and we are not! Who are we to argue or challenge the Almighty? If He wants to give me this thorn in my flesh called mental illness, then so be it. I have to look at it as a divine opportunity that God has given me to tell people about my wonderful Jesus and how He has made it possible for me to persevere through this awful disease. He has been my solid rock, my foundation, the only one who can give me the hope I need when I can't get off the floor. Who but Jesus can possibly fill this role?

I have one goal in life and that is to bring glory to the One who created me. One of my favorite Scripture verses is Proverbs 3:5–6, "Trust in the Lord with all your heart and lean not on your own understanding; in all your ways acknowledge Him and He will make you paths straight." Jesus has taken my crooked paths and made them straight. There was a popular song out a while back, and I loved it for this one line in the song. It said, "God bless the broken road that led me straight to you." I am thankful for my rocky road because it led me to the best thing that's ever happened to me. It led me to make the most important decision of my life. I will be rejoicing in this decision when the, "time for everything" comes.

As I look in the rearview mirror, I can see all the good that has come out of my mental illness. I have been able to write a book that hopefully will encourage people. I have been able to put myself out there and become a strong advocate for mental health. I get the pleasure of talking to people and freeing them from the misconception that they are alone in their fight and are too weak to make themselves better. I am not embarrassed to talk about my family and the addictions and suicides. If people see I'm not ashamed, then maybe they will let go of theirs. If I am able to offer hope to any one of my fellow sufferers, I will gladly bare my soul.

I have a simple question for you as you ponder this chapter about goals and seasons and making important decisions in your life. What or who are you living for? What is the foundation you are building your life upon? The children's story, "The Three Little Pigs," has a great spiritual analogy. Two of the pigs chose shoddy unstable foundations for their houses, and they were easily destroyed when the first big storm blew in. The wise pig built his house on a solid concrete foundation that could withstand anything that came against it. He was smart and knew he needed solid reinforcement when the big bad wolf called again. If we lay Jesus as our firm foundation, we will be able to withstand anything life throws at us, as well as fend off that big bad wolf called the devil. Are you like the wise pig, or are you content taking a chance on the destructible house?

CHAPTER 12

God's Will

MANY YEARS AGO, in my weekly Bible Study class, I learned something of great value that I could instantly apply to my life. It has stuck with me for over forty years. The teacher that day was talking about prayer and how God never lets any prayer go unanswered. As you can imagine, there were a few raised hands in the class mine being the first. "Wait a minute, I began. What do you mean? I've had lots of prayers that went unanswered." She went on to explain that God has one of four answers to every one of our prayers: yes, no, it's not the right time, or I have a better plan for you. It was the last one that impacted me the most. I never considered that if a prayer went unanswered that maybe, just maybe, God had something better in store for me. I also found out through experience that sometimes, God, answering my prayers, isn't necessarily a good thing.

I once prayed a prayer as a young adult that God by giving me. He gave me the desire of my heart. He allowed me to exercise my freewill and make a choice that was clearly not in my best interest. It actually turned out to be more than a bad judgment call, but it came with a life altering consequence. Consequences are necessary to help us make better choices in the future. One of the best questions to ask yourself when you're trying to make a decision is this. Just one question and it is this, "In light of my past, present, and future, is this decision I'm about to make the right one for me?" I wish I would have asked myself that question before moving ahead with my own agenda back then.

It must also be said that we will not always like God's answers to our prayers. The answer was not what we expected (they never are), and so we rebel or disregard the answer we were given. We sometimes may even give God some attitude because we were disappointed and feel like He let us down. God has a reason for everything. He does not act haphazardly or without purpose. We aren't supposed to understand everything God does in our lives. But we are called to have faith and trust in what God is doing. Our response to prayers that aren't answered the way we want should always be respected and accepted. God is always right. No matter what!

I don't yet understand everything that's happened to me nor am I supposed to. I most likely won't get any answers until I cross those pearly gates one day and have that first conversation with Jesus. I may not even care about answers at that point because I will finally be staring into the face of my Savior. I am so grateful that He's taught me how I can have peace with my disease. I've not only been able to accept it but excel in it.

A pastor once asked his congregation a very poignant question on a Sunday morning. He said, "If God never does another good thing for you, will you still love Him and serve Him?" If God doesn't take away your mental illness, are you still going to remain faithful to Him? Or is your love for Him conditional and predicated on the blessings He bestows on you? These are true thought-provoking questions that can be used for evaluating your spiritual life. The other parts of your life (physical and emotional) won't come together unless your spiritual life is on the right track. This is the basis of fulfillment for every other aspect of your life.

Part of God's will for me is to give my testimony about the secret weapon I have to battle mental illness. I can promise you with my whole heart and soul that Jesus can make it a whole lot easier for you to fight your battle if you invite Him to walk alongside you. He promises in His Word that He will go into the battle before us and have the victory. If you want to have the victory over your disease, you must enlist God's help, or you will struggle for the rest of your days.

I heard a story one time that really impacted me. It's about a farmer and a donkey. The farmer got mad at the donkey one day and threw him into a well. The farmer threw a shovel of dirt down on him day after day. However, day after day, the old donkey was determined in his quest and shook off the dirt, tamping it down under his feet. This went on for a while until one day, the farmer was in for a huge surprise. When he came out and grabbed his shovel of dirt and walked over to the well he found himself eye to eye with the braying beast. The donkey had tamped down all the soil so he would rise back up to the top. Can you imagine the look on that farmer's face?

What a lesson in perseverance. If the donkey had done nothing but stand there, he would have been buried in that well. But instead, he chose to fight back and do something about his situation. He kept stamping and stamping all that dirt down, fighting his way back up. His persistence certainly paid off as he had success and the farmer's plan backfired. There is a spiritual analogy to this story. Think of the farmer as the devil and us as the donkey. The devil is trying to bury us every day to separate us from God (which is always his ultimate goal) But we have the strength and power through Jesus to fight back, to stand up, and face our enemy just like the old nag. God wasn't done with that donkey yet. He would probably soon find himself with a new farmer being loved and appreciated like never before.

CHAPTER 13

Color My World

I HAVE BEEN totally sucked into the current coloring craze. I have always loved to color, and it's always the first thing I suggest when the grandkids show up. I don't care if it's Mickey Mouse or Superheroes count me in. However, as they grew up, games and Legos became more interesting, so I was left high and dry with my crayons. So, I was really excited when adult coloring books made their debut. I even went all in and invested some serious money in good coloring pencils.

My four children hit the jackpot when I picked up this new hobby. They no longer had to agonize over, "What should we get Mom for her birthday?" (Christmas, anniversary, fill in the blank) I couldn't stand it when they would hound me about gift ideas. I honestly could not finish the sentence, "I wish I had _____" (fill in the blank again). As long as I had Jesus, I had all I wanted or needed in life!

I started receiving coloring books of every style and genre for every occasion from there on out. I finally had to tell them to dial it back a notch as I had enough books to last me till the other side of heaven. But I wanted them to know I appreciated them, so I had to step up my game and really crank some pictures out. So, I stopped researching web.md in the evenings for the cause of my newest ache and pain and quit checking Facebook to see what someone else was having for dinner and instead began coloring. My husband liked my new hobby because I stopped complaining about his choice of television viewing, and we were both happy campers.

I was like a little kid, showing off my pictures to the family. I held them up for inspection and was always greeted with a, "Wow, (honey, mom, mimi), you did a great job. Nice choice of colors." I started to feel pretty proud of myself from all the accolades and began thinking of how I could use this newfound talent of mine to bless others. It came to me while walking on the treadmill one day that I could frame them and give them away as gifts. I tried a few out around the house, and they looked beautiful. So, I decided to start framing some favorites and handing them out. They were a huge hit because they were pretty as well as personal.

I discovered something whenever I was coloring. I felt very relaxed, and I could get totally lost in what I was doing. It took my mind off of everything else except what color scheme to choose for my picture (flowers with Scripture verses are my favorite). I noticed how immensely therapeutic it was. As I thought more about it, I realized how this could be used as mental health therapy. It is the perfect way to take your mind off of yourself and focus on something else. Then I thought that it didn't have to be coloring to be therapeutic. It could be whatever you enjoy doing—knitting, quilting, crafts, writing. Maybe you have a story inside of you that is waiting to be written. Or maybe you've always had a desire to take up painting or dance or playing the piano.

Anything that you can throw yourself into that will take the focus off yourself and channel it into a worthwhile interest or hobby is the goal. For me, writing has always been a passion. I wrote sappy poetry as a teenager and excelled in my creative writing classes in high school and college. Many years ago, I also started journaling when I was having my quiet time and fell in love with talking to God through a pen and paper. So far, I have filled thirty-five journals and still going strong. One day, God gave me the task of condensing some of those journals into a book, so I could publish them.

My writing hobby had soon turned into a huge project that I wasn't too sure I wanted to continue. God didn't give up though, so I soon found myself writing a yearly devotional. It took me three years filled with frustrations and setbacks, but we (God and I) were finally able to finish it and get it published. It's called, "But God," because of all the times, those two words are mentioned in the Bible when someone finds themselves in an impossible situation. But God steps in and works everything out perfectly.

I have another hobby, which isn't a great one, but I enjoy it and it relaxes me. Okay, I'm about to confess to you one of my biggest temptations that I indulge in way too much. I love to shop. My husband tells people I have a revolving closet as he never sees the same thing on me twice. Of course, he is totally exaggerating I tell him as I am cutting the price tag off of the new blouse I just put on. I do have my boundaries. I do not buy expensive things, and I only buy them if they're on sale. I have a shopping partner too. God is right there with me, helping me pick and choose. If I hold a blouse up for perusal, He reminds me that I already have a similar one hanging in my closet. He keeps me in check, but I still get to enjoy the hunt for the newest bargain. Little to my knowledge, however, I was on track for a major intervention as I made my way to meet a friend for shopping and lunch one day.

I had a dear friend that I met one day a week for lunch and shopping. We would have a nice lunch together, which always included something sinfully rich for dessert. Afterward, we would venture to the mall or TJ Maxx, which was our favorite. We could shop for hours. We seemed to never tire of it. And of course, I usually added a little something, albeit inexpensive, to my revolving closet.

As we were having lunch that day and discussing what stores we wanted to hit up, I heard the Lord whisper, "So is this how you are going to use the resources I've given you and the time that I've allotted you on this earth?" "Say what, Lord?" Surely I didn't understand what He was saying or asking me. Could it really be that I was being convicted of my spending habits and of squandering His precious gift of time? The answer was a resounding yes. I was in fact being called on the carpet for how I was handling my checkbook and my calendar.

The intervention was a success. I was guilty on all charges. So, it was obviously apparent that I had to find something more productive to do with my time and my money. But I didn't know what. So, I prayed about it, and again, I heard that still small voice whisper, "How about making those fleece blankets you like to make and donating them to Children's Hospital?" *Wow*, I thought, *God could be on to something.*

I had helped another friend at one time get through a horrible ordeal when her young son was diagnosed with cancer. He was in and out of the hospital and spent a fair amount of time in the infusion center, receiving chemo. When I went to visit, one of the things I noticed was how cold it was in the rooms and how thin the hospital blankets were on the beds. Bingo! It was like a light bulb flashed in my head, and I immediately thought of those fleece blankets.

And so it began. I spent two hours at the fabric store every month, picking out fleece in all sorts of fun patterns from princesses to dinosaurs. I would pile fifteen bolts of fabric at a time in my cart and head precariously to the cutting counter. Watching people's faces when they caught sight of my cart was always fun. You could visibly see their relief when they got to the counter ahead of me.

The nurses later told me that the kids loved their blankets so much that they took them home and then brought them back the next time they came in for treatment. One day, I had a lady approach me as I was standing in line with my mountain of fleece and ask me what I was doing with all that material. When I told her, her face lit up, and she excitedly replied, "You won't believe this, but my son had leukemia and was in the infusion center when one day a nurse came in and handed him one of your blankets. He is ten now, and he still keeps that blanket on his bed." Being at the mall couldn't possibly compare to the joy that conversation brought me that day. I was investing in someone other than myself and it felt really good.

Hopefully, you have gotten some good insight into how valuable hobbies can be for fighting mental illness as well as exercising your creative side. Also, I hope you've seen the importance of giving to others and the contribution you can make to the world. Are you asking yourself at this point what hobbies you can use to take your mind off of your disease? Are you unsure of what the possibilities might even be? Ask yourself these questions: What do you think you're good at or have a special bend towards? What kinds of things are you naturally drawn to or that excite you? What qualities have other people seen in you and commented on? Think of ways you can turn these interests into blessings. Nursing homes are another great option for donating handcrafted items. Pictures to hang on their walls, shawls, even the donation of your time is a perfect way of giving back to the community.

I recently took my granddaughter on a field trip to a nursing home. We were able to sit and color and play games with them. It was so much fun, and they were all smiles. The children then sang some songs in the cafeteria, and I've never seen so many happy faces. They clapped and clapped when they were all finished. I would have to say that they thoroughly enjoyed our visit and the love we shared with them.

I have two friends who love to organize. They go into people's homes and clean out a closet or organize a room. The before and after pictures are truly amazing. I have another friend who volunteers at the Food Bank at her church, organizing all the donations that come in. She absolutely loves it. She stocks the shelves and fills orders, and sometimes, she even delivers the food. She tells me she feels so blessed to be able to do these things for others.

One of my high-energy friends pushes wheelchairs at the airport, getting people from gate to gate (this is a paying job that she has turned into a ministry). She adores her job because it allows her to get in some exercise as well as meet and talk to people. She told me it is a great opportunity for her to live out her faith by showing kindness and love. I asked her if she talked to the people about her faith. She answered, "Well how about this for a conversation starter—so tell me, what has God done in your life this week? You will be amazed at the answers you get and how easy it is to keep the dialogue going from there."

Yes, it's hard to want to be around other people when you're feeling down and out. It's so easy to become a recluse when you're in the pit. We like to isolate ourselves because it's just easier than having to deal with the world. I've been there many times. But luckily, I had a husband and friends who would pull me out of the house and insist I go to lunch or dinner or sometimes even a movie. They knew that I needed to get out and get my mind off of my suffering. God never intended for us to be islands. Jesus surrounded Himself with twelve men the entire three years of His ministry. Even He knew He couldn't go it alone. We were created to be in relationship with people, Jesus being the most important of all. Life is meant to be shared especially during the hard times.

It's also a good idea to spend some time educating yourself about your disease so that when you do talk to people, you have a good foundation of knowledge. I have a brother that gets frustrated with me when I try and talk to him about my disease, so I just tell him to go research it for himself. Our families also have to be aware and really understand what we have and what we're going through. There is some really good informative sights out there. The NIMH (National Institute of Mental Health) gives a plethora of information and statistics. There are explanations for every kind of mental illness. There are also some great books that can be helpful.

When my son was diagnosed with bipolar disorder, I went to the bookstore (back before Amazon) and bought one of those popular "Dummies" books called *Bipolar Disorder for Dummies*. It was written without all the medical jargon, so it was very easy to read and understand. It was a great way to get a basic understanding of the disease and the treatment options. And as I mentioned earlier, the special Mental Health edition of Time Magazine's July 2019 issue is one of the best resources I've ever come across.

You are definitely *not* alone in your battle with this disease. According to the NIMH, mental illness is the number one cause of disability in our country. We are in the throes of a full-blown epidemic of mental illness like we've never experienced before. Don't ever think you're alone in your pain and suffering, my friends. We are among millions of people who suffer with this disease.

CHAPTER 14

Vitamin D

I LIVE WHERE some people travel to for vacation. I live on the Florida Panhandle where the beaches are known for their sugar white sand and Caribbean teal colored waters. You would think that since I live in this little slice of paradise that I would frequent those beautiful beaches and soak up all that Vitamin D. Truth is, I don't like the beach. Or the sun. Most of all, I can't stand the sand because—well—it's sand! I can't stand walking in it, lying on it, swimming with it, and worst of all, being covered in it.

I won't even mention the anxiety it gives me when it gets in the car, the house, the towels, my bathing suit, and my hair (I could go on). A windy day turns it into a swirling tornado, leaving pockmarks on your skin as it pelts your body. When the grandkids mention going to the beach, I always find an excuse not to go. I love them, but I have my boundaries. Why would I want to go to the beach when I have a nice sand-free swimming pool in my backyard?" God didn't like sand either or He would have put Adam and Eve seaside versus in a garden!

You will never find one dermatologist who thinks the sun is good for you. Did you know that if you put sunscreen on, it totally blocks all that good Vitamin D our bodies need? I live in the Sunshine state, and believe it or not, I am deficient in Vitamin D and have to take it in capsule form. I am very fair-skinned and get teased a lot because I don't sport the usual Florida tan. "How can you live in Florida and look like Casper the Ghost?" A suntan never appealed to me mostly because I found lying in the sun torture. Who enjoys sweat, oozing from every pore, and your skin being baked to a crisp? No thanks.

I'm a northern girl and always will be. When I lived in Pennsylvania, I loved the different seasons. Fall was my absolute favorite. I was in awe as mid-October rolled around, and all the colors exploded on the trees. One morning, as I was taking a walk, I was genuinely caught up in the beauty of creation. I thought what a wonderfully creative God we have! Richly colored leaves are just the tip of the iceberg when it comes to the spectacular world God gave us to live in.

Did you know there are spiritual lessons in all of nature? The Bible tells us, "First the natural then the spiritual" (1 Cor. 15:46). On one particular walk in this cascade of color, I was struck with a spiritual analogy. I looked at the trees with their breathtaking display of leaves and thought about the seasons and how much our lives mimic them. Just like the farmer reaps his crops in the fall, we have times of harvest in our lives where we get to share with others what God has brought forth in our lives. The seeds of faith that were planted in us at one time are now mature and ready to be gathered in. We are in our season of fruitfulness as a result of all our hard work. It's a plentiful season of our faith.

Just as the winter season can be cold and miserable, we may experience similar hardships in this corresponding spiritual season. The landscape looks bleak and barren, and our faith seems to be in that same condition. These are seasons where our faith may be tested. We may have to be still and wait just like the dead lifeless trees in winter wait for the first whiff of spring.

Spring is a wonderful time of year when Mother Nature brings the earth to life again. Everything looks fresh and new. Vibrant hues of green are sprouting everywhere you look. Our spiritual springs are just like that. Our difficult circumstances take a breather, and the sun shines one again. This is also the planting season in nature and in the spiritual sense. Seeds are scattered over the fertile ground, and the earth receives them and causes them to take root. It's the same way in our hearts. If we allow seeds of faith to be planted in the soil of our hearts, our faith will deepen and grow. We will have a newfound hope like never before when all those seeds start to bloom. Our faith will start exploding like the cascades of color on a beautiful spring day.

Summer is the season where all of creation is in its glory and ready to enjoy. Mother Nature sits back and enjoys her Sabbath just as God rested on the seventh day so He could sit back and enjoy all that He had made. He wants us to do the same in our summer season. He allows us to have seasons of refreshment from the demands of life, so we can be prepared for what's ahead. God knows our need for relaxation and gives us these seasons to have fun and enjoy. I am a leader in BSF (Bible Study Fellowship) and we meet from September to May. It's a weekly commitment and involves a fair amount of time. When summer comes, I get to kick back and put the lessons and homework aside (but never the Bible reading). I enjoy the summer break so I will be prepared in the fall to be the best leader I can be when we reconvene.

All seasons require sunshine just like we do. Sunlight is a key tool in the battle with mental illness. It's been proven that light affects our moods. I noticed that when I moved to Florida from one of the cloudiest cities in the country, my depression seemed to respond positively. I didn't feel so blah all the time. I had more energy and the desire to get out more and do things. It's much more enticing to get out of the house when the sun is shining than when it's gray and gloomy.

Seasonal affective disorder (SAD) is real and well documented. We naturally respond to sunshine as it feeds our bodies the nutrients it needs. When I lived in the north, and the sun was AWOL most of the winter, I took advantage of the days when it happened to grace us with its presence. I would pull a chair under a window and sit where the sun streamed in. Just like a dog basking in the sun, I sat soaking it up through my window. Getting in the sun without sunscreen for twenty minutes a day will boost your mood as well as keep that Vitamin D feeding your brain.

The fresh air is rejuvenating as well. A radio jockey back in the day used to say, "Smile. The fresh air is good for your teeth." My mother used to tell me to be sure to take my babies outside because the fresh air was good for them. In England, back in the '50s mothers used to park their babies in their prams outside their front doors for some fresh air while they went and did housework. Following Mom's orders, I did take my babies outside, and it was truly amazing how it calmed them down. One of my grandbabies was a particularly fussy bundle of joy, but as soon as I took her out in the fresh air, she would stop crying and usually fall asleep. Now I tell my children the same thing my mother told me. Strolling a baby in the open air is not only good for the wee one, but it also gives mom a chance to enjoy nature and get some exercise.

We are just bigger versions of babies. Light and fresh air can do wonders for us as well. You will reap the reward if you take the time to get out and soak up some of God's glorious sunshine. If you live where the sun is a figment of your imagination, you might want to invest in a sun lamp. It truly does make a difference.

CHAPTER 15

Love Me Some HGTV

I AM AN HGTV junkie. Whether it's "Love it or List it," or remodeling a fixer-upper, I'm giddy with anticipation. I could literally watch it for hours (and I have). I dream of the Property Brothers, knocking on my front door one day and asking if I would be interested in a home renovation. I already know exactly what they need to do. I've got it all planned out.

I justify my obsession with HGTV by putting my treadmill right in front of the TV. I figure it kills two birds with one stone. It's a win/win. I love my treadmill because I like to walk, and I actually like to sweat all the impurities out of my body. To be clear, I love exercise sweat just not that nasty beach sweat. A good workout also cleanses my mind, and I'm able to focus better. It gives me the oomph I need to start the day. There is nothing like exercise to make you feel like you've accomplished something and make you feel good about yourself. I notice that when I miss a couple days in a row, I immediately feel it in my mood. A sluggishness sets in, and I don't feel like moving. I feel, for lack of a better word, "yucky." My family starts calling me cranky pants, which sends the grandkids into fits of laughter.

Exercise is vital when it comes to depression. Any physician will tell you it is a big part of the treatment process. Working out your body produces endorphins in the brain which are the feel-good hormones. Have you ever talked to anyone after they've worked out and they tell you they feel worse than when they started? Or that they wished they hadn't worked out at all? I've been in plenty of gyms through the years, and I've never met anyone who regrets having exercised.

It doesn't matter what kind of exercise you choose. You can't go wrong as far as your brain is concerned. The results far outweigh any aches and pains you may experience. Try and make it a part of your daily routine even if just for fifteen minutes. You will be amazed at the difference it makes to those chemicals dancing around in your head.

I got my fair share of exercise one day while vacationing in another city. I must preface this story with the fact that even though I am fairly adept at exercise, my geographical skills don't quite measure up. I got on the interstate one day in Pittsburgh heading to Ohio, and an hour and a half later, found myself in a small ski resort in the middle of Pennsylvania. I kept wondering why I wasn't seeing any, "Welcome to Ohio," signs. My family has never let me live that one down.

This particular morning, my husband was out golfing, so I decided to take a walk and see the sights. The way the hotel was situated, I thought if I just started walking to the right, I would loop back around and wind my way back to my starting point. Like a circle I imagined. So, I set out from the hotel in my glory, enjoying the sunshine and scenery. However, it dawned on me after a while that I was not rounding any corners like I expected but was just walking in a straight line. I saw no side streets to make a turn. I stopped to try and get my bearings but of course that was futile. I can't tell north from south or east from west. So, I just continued walking thinking I would eventually find a corner.

About thirty minutes later, I started to get a little concerned (and hot). I felt like I was in the middle of nowhere as there was not a car nor a human in sight. I knew I must be off the beaten path though I knew not how or where. Finally, a cyclist appeared out of nowhere (an angel in bike shorts and helmet) and I flagged him down. The conversation went something like this, "The Hilton? Oh, you passed that a ways back, miles ago. Go back about two miles take the cycle path to the left and then it's about two miles down on your right."

Needless to say, my walk turned into an unplanned marathon that day, but like all of our challenging experiences, I learned a good lesson. Always grab a map before setting out in unchartered territory. Of course, it would have done me no good because I can't read maps either. I would have just stared at it like a Chinese menu and scratched my head. God gave me many gifts but a sense of direction was not one of them.

Incorporating some type of exercise in your day will do wonders for both your body and your mind. When I walk outside, I always use that time to appreciate God's beautiful creation as well as talk to Him just like I'm walking alongside a friend. Which I am. God calls us his friends in the Bible. He wants us to be open and intimate with Him just like we would with our best buddy. I love that I can talk to Him about anything without any judgment or condemnation. His love for us is unconditional. We can't do or say anything that would make Him love us any more or any less than He already does. That is so very comforting to me as I mess up quite frequently. Thank God for His unending grace and forgiveness. He truly is an Awesome God.

CHAPTER 16

The Blue Smock

THE BLUE SMOCK is one of the most important weapons you have in the mental illness arsenal. I also learned another wonderful attribute of God in this next story. He has a great sense of humor.

Before retirement, I made a promise to myself that I would never be one of those gray-haired old ladies in hospital gift shops, wearing one of those tacky blue smocks. Or sitting at the information desk in the lobby, dishing out directions to other geographically challenged people like me. That just wasn't my thing I smugly remember thinking to myself.

When my husband retired, we moved to Pensacola, Florida. I was not a happy camper. I was born and raised in the north and was a true Yankee. To say I was homesick is a huge understatement. As you might imagine, I came down with a nasty case of the "feeling sorry for myself blues." Change is a huge stressor, especially for those of us who suffer with mental illness. In retrospect, I think I could have handled it a bit better by utilizing some of the tools I'm talking about in this book. It's always more challenging for the teacher to follow her instructions than her students. Unfortunately, a storm was brewing, and a huge depressive episode was on the horizon.

To make matters worse, I hadn't had a chance to find a new doctor yet. Psychiatrists, at least where I live, are hard to find—much less try to book an appointment. One highly recommended doctor had me fill out a rather lengthy questionnaire before I could be "accepted" into the practice. They asked me everything but my shoe size. I didn't hear back, so I called to see if I passed the test and the secretary said, "No, Mrs. Kelly, your case is too extensive and wouldn't be a good fit for the doctor." I was stunned to say the least. And angry. Are you kidding me? *Can doctors even do that?* I wondered. Does this ever happen in cases where a person is physically sick? Do doctors turn patients down because they're not a "good fit?" This is another example of the prejudice that exists with mental illness.

When I finally did locate a new doctor, one of the things he suggested was to get involved in some volunteer work. He said it would help alleviate my depression as well as I would get to meet new people. He suggested I try one of the local hospitals. *Okay*, I thought, *I can go rock some sweet little babies in the nursery.* That would be fun.

So, I called one of the hospitals and went in for an interview. "Well," the director began, "the only openings we have at the moment are in the gift shop." I almost choked.

"No babies?" I sputtered.

"No," she said, "those positions fill up the fastest."

Oh, brother, now what was I going to do. I couldn't just say no thanks and get up and leave. So I hesitantly and with bated breath asked her, "What color are the smocks you have to wear in the gift shop?"

She brightly responded, "Oh, they are a beautiful shade of royal blue!"

A week later, I found myself in a lovely blue smock slinging candy and chewing gum behind the counter of the hospital gift shop. My husband found it hysterical as I put that smock on when I headed out the door. I found little humor in the situation. But I decided to go with it, put the best smile I could on my face, and let my Jesus light shine. Sometimes it just takes putting a smile on your face to make you feel better. It wasn't long before I actually started enjoying myself. I'm a people person at heart, so I loved interacting with the customers. I teased the valet guys as they came in and out all day to chat and pick up one more Snickers.

I became friendly with one of the valets in particular who was one of my best customers. He would stand there for fifteen minutes at the counter with me, and we would just gab away. I kept wondering about the cars that were backing up outside but he didn't seem to care much. We got talking about faith one day and reading the Bible, and he commented that he didn't own a Bible. It was my great pleasure and honor to be able to buy him his first Bible and give it to him the following week. It was like I had handed this young man a thousand dollars. His face lit up, and he thanked me every time I saw him from then on. The joy I received from this experience actually made me start to like my blue smock.

I ended up working in that Gift shop for five years until my granddaughter was born, and I became a full-time Mimi and found myself up to my ears in diapers again. I hung my blue smock up with a great feeling of accomplishment. I kept it in my closet for years to remind myself of a valuable lesson God taught me. First, doing something you don't want to do will always bring reward. Second, interacting with people is good for us and takes the focus off of our problems. I never once thought about my depression the whole time I was in that gift shop. I was having too much fun.

Hospital gift shops aren't the only places for volunteer opportunities. Your local church most likely can provide you with a list of areas where they need help inside and outside of the church. Most churches have outreaches where you can get involved in for instance feeding programs, tutoring, school programs, helping the shut-ins, all sorts of possibilities. I enjoyed my volunteer experience so much that I signed up to be a greeter at my church. All it required was to hold a door open while extending a hand, a hug, or a warm smile on Sunday mornings. It not only served a need in the church, but it allowed me to meet and greet many new people some of whom I've become good friends with. Even the days I wanted to stay home, I made myself go because I knew how much better I would feel later. Sometimes, if you just put the smile on first, the feeling will naturally come with it.

There are so many opportunities for giving back to the world. Jesus came to earth not to be served but to serve others. His focus was solely on people and never His own needs. He was all about relationships as He healed, loved, encouraged, and put others before

Himself. Serving can transform our lives. I heard a pastor say one time that "the greatest joy in life is serving God and others." In retrospect, I think he was right on! Jesus didn't wear a blue smock, but He was by far the greatest volunteer who ever lived!

If you're not sure where you want to plug in as a volunteer, pray and ask God to show you what would be a good fit for you. Ask Him to open the doors that He wants you to walk through. He opened the door of that gift shop when I least expected or wanted it. But look at all the good that came out of it. God hears our every prayer, and He always knows what's best for us. He knows where you will bloom. You just have to ask Him to lead you to it.

CHAPTER 17

If I Had a Hammer

MY FOUR-YEAR-OLD GRANDSON has had a love affair with tools since he was two years old. He would follow his dad out to the garage at every chance and work right alongside him on whatever project he was working on. A lawn mower, leaf blower, or even a ladder would throw him over the edge of excitement. Of course, he had to have his own toy mower and would follow right behind his daddy with his little mower happier than Peppa pig in a muddy puddle.

If you really wanted to make his day, you took him for a spin over to Lowe's or Home Depot. He was in his glory just, walking down the aisles, and looking at all the tools and gadgets. When dad bought something, he acted like it was Christmas morning, and he just hit pay dirt.

One fateful morning, however, the little guy was on a mission. He found daddy's big boy hammer, lying forgotten in the living room. The wheels started turning, and he went in search of something to practice on. It was then that his keen little eye caught one of mom's brand-new acquisitions. She happened to make the fatal mistake of leaving her Apple watch within arms' reach on the kitchen counter. The little imp also happened to notice that mom had left the room for a quick shower. He hit the lotto. He reached up to the counter, grabbed the watch, and placed it flat out on the floor. He had sniper accurate aim and hit his target dead on. As he was pleased with this first success, he then set his sights on the ceramic tile on the fireplace hearth. It looked pretty inviting as well so again he raised the hammer up and slammed it down on the tile. This sound of course brought the matter to my daughter's attention and well let's just say a rather tense situation ensued. Luckily for the preservation of the household, his tool obsession moved onto dinosaurs, and T-Rex then claimed his total affections.

I am a girly girl (always have been) and know absolutely nothing about anything in the garage except how to use a ladder. I couldn't tell you the difference between a bolt and a nut. The first time my husband asked me for a Phillips head screwdriver, I looked for someone else in the room because I knew he couldn't be talking to me. "You know, honey, the one with the rounded pointy end." I didn't even know there were different types of screwdrivers, so at least I was beginning to build my tool knowledge.

I may not know a lot about Craftsman tools, but I think I am pretty familiar at this point in my life with spiritual tools. I have been taught by a good and faithful God how to use these tools to battle my mental illness, and I'm hoping that they will be useful for you too. I have based this entire book on the first bullet point below.

- Jesus! He is my ultimate secret weapon for fighting my disease. Nothing or no one else could have had a more positive impact on me or provided me with the ongoing perseverance I needed to soldier on. I can tell you with the utmost sincerity that I owe my life to Him. To be clear, I am not just referring to faith here. I'm talking about having a personal relationship with the One who gave His life for us. Jesus died and rose again, so that we may share eternal life with Him in heaven. Just as you say "I do" to one person in a marriage and are committed to them for a lifetime so it is with Jesus. When we say 'I do" to Him, we have committed our entire lives to Him. We have promised to love and follow Him all the days of our lives. He then promises never to leave nor forsake us, and He goes to prepare a room for us in heaven.

Have you made that commitment to Jesus yet? Do you know with absolute certainty whether your room in heaven is reserved? This might be a good time to stop and think about these questions as they are the only questions in life that truly matter. It is only our pride that prevents us from giving control of our lives over to God. We think we are quite capable of doing life on our own and don't need any help. We tell ourselves that we don't have to rely on anyone, that we are perfectly self-sufficient. I have one question. How's that working out for you? Please believe me, friends, as I speak from years and years of experience. Jesus is the hope you've been crying out for and have not yet been able to find. He is that hole in your heart that you can never seem to fill. He is the secret weapon you need to successfully live with your mental illness

- Roll baby roll. The second most important thing I have learned is to roll with my disease. My favorite encouragement to myself is simply, "It is what it is." I gave up trying to change what I can't change a long time ago. I have accepted that I have mental illness and that it will probably follow me around for the rest of my life. But that's okay. I will roll with it and take the hits as they come. I know that I am not alone in this battle and neither are you. I can't pull that thorn of suffering out of my side, but I have someone beside me who can ease the pain and make it bearable. Learning how to roll with your illness and not buck it will be revolutionary in how you live day to day.

- It's okay to be selfish! Every disease has its limitations whether physically or mentally. A pitfall for those suffering with mental illness is busyness. Thinking you have to do it all or have it all is so detrimental to your mental health. Signing up for every ministry at church, event planning at work, or being super mom and taking charge of all the class parties has red flags all over it. This added stress is lethal to mental illness sufferers. I call this elective stress as we are choosing to fill our plates to overflowing. Any extra activity you sign up for has the potential to affect your mood and attitude. I am not trying to scare you away from any of these well-intentioned volunteer opportunities I am only speaking from my own experiences. Having an over full plate will most assuredly compromise your mental well-being. I feel bad sometimes saying no to things that people ask me to do, but I have learned that for the sake of my sanity and the well-being of my family, I have to decline. It's no different than having a physical restriction that prevents you from being actively involved. Why should mental illness be any different?

- Shake off those insensitive remarks. This is an absolute must. Refuse to take on the guilt and shame society wants to put on you. Don't let others try to insinuate that this disease is somehow your fault. Or it's just a weakness that you have to overcome. This is pure nonsense spoken out of ignorance. You have absolutely nothing to feel ashamed about. You are no different than a person with any other disease. I have developed a boldness over the years because of my passion for mental health awareness. I confront those people who so easily toss out insensitive remarks and educate them on the facts. I suggest they do some research so they can develop a respect for mental illness and the compassion it rightfully deserves.

- Think outside the box. If we focus on others, we will have less time to think about what we may be going through. There is nothing worse for mental illness sufferers than to have too much time on their hands. I know that sounds a bit contradictory to what I just said above but it's all about balance. There is a happy medium between the two. Our calendars should reflect healthy involvements. We must exercise discernment when it comes to filling up our day-timers. Being inactive sometimes contributes to a "poor me" attitude, which will accentuate how down we feel. It might take a step of faith to approach outside opportunities but they will help you more than you can imagine. If it becomes too great a burden, you can always scale back or decide it's not right for you. Trying is the important thing. Sometimes, you have to face a fear to overcome it. I have to remind myself when I experience doubt that fear is the opposite of faith.

- Take a deep breath. Being still is a command in the Bible, i.e., naps are not just for babies! Rest is very important for those with mental illness particularly when you're having a hard day. Rest is a great way of decompressing and rejuvenating. I am not ashamed to admit that I probably nap three to four days a week. I don't mean one of those twenty-minute cat naps either. I mean an hour at least. I know this is an impossible feat for some because of jobs or little ones. But if your child is asleep, it might be a good idea to follow suit.

  When my grandkids are over for the day, they actually look forward to Mimi's naptime. We lay down together on my bed, and while I read or nap, they lie beside me and watch TV, read, or play on their tablets. Fatigue adds fuel to the fire of depression, so we must always do our best to keep ourselves caught up on our rest. I also don't mind admitting that I go to bed around eight o'clock every night. Granted I have the luxury to do that because of being retired, but I know what I need and I require a lot of sleep. Friends and family know not to text or call me after dinner.

- Fill-ups. Be aware of what drains your tank! If you find social situations to be extremely taxing, it's okay to just go for a little while or even not go at all. I have had to decline many an invitation because I was not in the right frame of mind to go and mingle with people. It can be extremely painful when you have to be around people if you're not feeling up to it. It's not being selfish or copping out. If you weren't feeling well physically, you wouldn't want to be out and about. It's no different feeling mentally unwell. I speak from years of experience here too. I never allowed myself to feel guilty over events I had to miss.

Also, I found that spending time with negative people pulled me right down with them. I even had to give up some friendships because they drained me dry. I couldn't afford to add what I called "optional stress" to my life. Always remember that your mental health is more important than what other people might think about you. Their opinions don't matter. Just concentrate on keeping that tank of yours full.

- Be responsible. I have come across many people in my thirty-year journey with mental illness who say they forgot to take their meds or forgot to get the prescription refilled. Or they play around with dosages or go off their medication entirely. Some don't think they need it anymore, so they just stop taking it. My son who has bipolar is guilty of this. I have seen firsthand the problems it has caused in his life, some being extremely serious. Please, if you are put on medication, take it correctly. Altering the dosage can not only cause major setbacks, but it can cause the drug to not work when restarted. My adult children tell me today that they are proud of me because I took responsibility early on for my illness and have always followed doctor's orders. This is an essential point not just for mental illness but any disease. Take your medicine as prescribed and never go off of it without consulting your physician.

- Chat it up. Sometimes, the last thing you want to do with anyone when you're depressed is talk. It seems painful to have to talk to people when all we want is to be left alone. Again, this calls for a step of faith. I have found through the years that it is actually therapeutic when I talk to people about my disease. I've learned to get real honest and talk about my struggles openly. I've often wondered why there have never been any organized meetings instituted for mental illness like there are for alcoholics and drug addicts. Wouldn't it be great to have a place to go and vent our challenges and frustrations? Where we would feel safe and accepted in a room with other people dealing with the same issues. When we lean on each other, we have another pair of legs to hold us up when we need it.

- Free therapy. Sometimes, when I am struggling with a serious issue in my life, I think to myself, *Maybe I should go get some counseling*. As soon as the thought crosses my mind, I can sense God, saying, "What for? You already have the greatest counselor, living inside of you." True that. So when these issues pop up, I grab my Bible and my journal, and I write all my feelings down on paper and then ask God to share His wisdom and insight with me. Sometimes, he will speak through a Scripture verse, and maybe another time, my answer or confusion will be cleared up through a conversation with a friend. This has happened to me on a number of occasions. And I know without a shadow of a doubt that God is giving me the advice I needed to hear. I came to the conclusion that writing can be very instrumental in sorting out my feelings as well as making me aware of something I need to address. God has a way of gently letting us see what areas in our lives we need to work on. However, He is never condemning. If you feel that way, be assured it is not coming from God. Romans 8:1 says, "For there is no condemnation for those who live in Christ Jesus."

Just as tears are very cleansing and cathartic, so is being honest with God. You can tell Him anything, and He will gladly listen. We can never tell God anything or do anything that would make Him love us anymore or any less than He does right at this very moment.

God and I work out my challenges and obstacles together. He is the only one who knows me inside and out and knows what's in my best interest. Why would I trust anyone else to get me through the storms of life? I consider this another powerful weapon we have at our disposal to battle mental illness. Pick up a pen and a notebook and try it.

CHAPTER 18

Why Me?

I RAN ACROSS a verse in the Old Testament as I was writing one day that God impressed upon me to use in a chapter of the book. The Scripture verse is found in Deuteronomy 23:5. It says, "But God turned the curse into a blessing for you." *Wow*, I thought, *this verse summed up my life pretty well*. God has turned what I saw as a curse in the beginning into a huge blessing because I can now offer hope to all those who suffer with the disease like me. He, in essence, gave me a ministry through my pain and suffering. He blessed me to be able to be a mental health advocate to speak up for the ones who need a voice. I believe it was God's plan all along. He was building a tremendous testimony in me that I would be able to share for the good of others. This, by the way, is always God's ultimate purpose in our struggles. No experience is ever wasted with God.

I definitely wouldn't have asked to live with such an affliction, but since it was not my choice, I had to (and you have to) learn how to live with it. I've suffered huge losses in my life, but God has given me the secret weapon that keeps me going day after day. He offers this secret weapon to you as well. All you have to do is receive it. It is only by the grace of God I am able to live a happy and fulfilled life. I live with great peace and joy because I have the best defense you can possibly have. This is my prayer for you my friend.

I have been involved in many Bible studies through the years (still am) and have made some great friends. I was having lunch with my eighty-six-year-old spiritual mama recently when she shared some wonderful words of wisdom. At eighty-six, you tend to sit up and listen when that many years of life experience speaks up. She said to me, "You know, Cori, we're supposed to suffer in this life. Jesus told us in His Word to expect it. So, why would we ever expect to live a trouble free life? Jesus certainly faced hardship. Are we any better than Him, or less deserving of the same treatment?"

As I thought about this later on, I recalled all the times in my past that I said to God, "You know, Lord, I really don't think I deserve... (fill in the blank). Don't you think I have been through enough heartbreaks? Can't you pick on someone else for a while?" I have told Him countless times in the past that something or other wasn't fair and that I shouldn't have to put up with any more pain and suffering. God knows our hearts better than we do, so I figured it was okay to be real with Him and lay it all out there.

A few weeks after that lunch, I had coffee with another friend, and God decided at this point to set me straight on a few things. Sometimes God has to intervene in our lives through other people to help us see more clearly. I was sharing my new trial with my friend and brought up the fact that I didn't think I really deserved to have to deal with this particular problem again. She stopped me dead in my tracks, looked me right in the eye, and said, "Hold on a minute, sister. What makes you think you deserve or don't deserve anything? The Bible never says that we deserve only happiness and good things. Did you seriously think life was going to be all sunshine and roses?"

Then to really drive her point home, she said, "Did Jesus, who was a totally innocent man, deserve to die? Did He deserve to be tortured and hung on a cross for crimes He never committed? No, He chose to do that. He needed to die so that we could live. He wanted to give us a life with Him after we take our final breath versus die condemned without ever reaching the pearly gates. He did that for us even though He didn't *deserve* it. And yet we complain that we shouldn't have to endure this or that and pray for Him to take it away."

I was really thankful my friend was being so honest with me and holding me accountable for my wrong thinking. I obviously needed to hear what she had to say. My friend continued to educate me on why we should not blame God when bad things happen. She continued, "God didn't cause your suffering. God is a good God and is not out to inflict pain or harm on anyone. The problem is we live in an evil, sinful world thanks to Adam and Eve. The Garden of Eden was a perfect place until man ruined it by disobeying God. Because of them, our world is far from what God intended."

Pain and suffering should be expected in this life, and we shouldn't be surprised when it rears its ugly head. The good news is that we are never left to deal with our problems alone. Jesus will always be right by our side, helping us get through our challenges. Personally, I can't even imagine trying to get through a trial in my life without Jesus beside me. There is absolutely no one else who could give me such unimaginable peace when my world is rocking. My only hope is through Jesus and Jesus alone.

I committed that day at lunch with my friend to never question God again about what I deserve or don't deserve. I don't ask God the "why" question any more. I simply ask Him to show me what I should be learning from the experience. I ask Him, "What is the lesson you want to teach me here, Lord?" Friends, I'm not saying that I rejoice when new trials come my way. We're not called to give thanks *for* our trials, but to find something *in* them to be thankful for. I know I can handle what He has given me because I *am* dealing with it. I am getting through it by His strength alone.

I was in the ER recently, experiencing tremendous back pain. According to my favorite website, Web MD, it said I most likely had a kidney stone. I was crying like a baby in pain. As I sat there, waiting (and waiting and waiting) to see a doctor, my husband suggested that I try to think of one thing to be thankful for. "Are you kidding me right now?" was my gracious reply. I knew he was just trying to get my mind off of the pain and onto something positive, but I thought his suggestion was utterly ridiculous. So, just to prevent him from any further unsolicited uplifting advice, I gave it a shot. *Okay,* I thought, *what is one thing I can be thankful for right now?* The only thing I could come up with was, "I guess it could be worse. Thank you, God, for not letting me spew my lunch everywhere." It is totally amazing what a little gratitude can do for an attitude.

If you are still tempted to ask that why question, think about this. What would it change if you knew the answer? It wouldn't change your circumstances nor would it change the outcome. I can assure you that God has already given us the answer to all of our why questions. The answer really boils down to one word and that is "Because. Because I am God and you are not." I don't believe that there has ever been a parent on this earth who hasn't given this same answer to their child. When I asked why about this or that when I was growing up, I was always told, "Because I said so." We don't like this answer from God any more than our kids liked it from us. If you are still shaking your fist at God asking Him that "why me" question, you now know the answer. Accepting where God has us in life is freeing ourselves up to enjoy life again.

CHAPTER 19

Existence vs. Life

CHANGE IS HARD. Any kind of change is a challenge. When my husband retired, we moved from the north to sunny Florida. We ditched our boots and invested in sandals and sunscreen. Leaving our winter coats behind, we headed off to the land of hurricanes and squelching heat. I wasn't all that convinced that this was a good move. I happened to like the three other seasons of the year. Christmas shopping in flip-flops amid palm trees laden with Christmas lights did nothing to put me in the holiday spirit.

However, the weather changes were the least of my worries when we moved south. Not only was I having to get used to heat that could fry eggs on the sidewalk, I was faced with a retired husband who was always underfoot. When our kids were young and he called and told me he was headed out for a round of golf, I would get upset because he was having fun, and I was home with four kids. Now, I push him out the door to the course with a big smile, a pat on the back, and a "have a great game, honey." Retirement convinced me that God never intended married couples to eat breakfast, lunch, and dinner together day in and day out.

With my husband's helpful advice, I learned that I had been loading the dishwasher wrong for forty years. He demonstrated the "right" way to do it as I sat back and made my tongue bleed. I also learned that I was not taking advantage of the proper drying cycle when I did the laundry. I actually discovered many things that I could improve upon around the house thanks to his retirement.

After months of trying to transition to my new helper, I realized I needed to get a grip. I knew I had to get rid of my Debbie Downer attitude and accept my plight. I knew I had to change my attitude or I was headed for much bigger trouble. I heard a sermon in church soon after this epiphany that perked up my ears. The pastor made the comment that "circumstance do not have to dictate your life." I was pretty sure God was speaking directly to me at that moment. I had a choice to make. I had to make an effort to change my way of thinking. I had to take my own advice and just learn to "roll with it." I couldn't change the circumstances but I could alter my reaction to them.

I think this is where some people with mental illness get stuck in their lives. They choose existence over really living. They get so comfortable in their dysfunctional situation that it begins to feel normal. They get used to feeling like things will never change so why bother. I have experienced these feelings many times through my years of depression. Life becomes so overwhelming that taking a seat on the bleachers is just easier. Living simply to exist is not really living. Existing is defined as enduring, surviving, to just be present.

I know people personally who find that participating in life is just too exhausting. Of course, when you're depressed, it's hard to get out of that mindset. Believe me, I get it. But it can be done. Not by any effort on your part though. That's the thing. It's really not your battle but God's. The Bible says that "apart from God you can do nothing." You have to employ that secret weapon I've been talking about to get you out of just existing to living life again. He is your only hope for a happy, fulfilled life.

I have a mission statement for my life that I like to share with people. Thinking about this reminded me of a story about bumper stickers. I have never had a bumper sticker on my car. No crosses. No fish. No family tree. No vote for… (fill in the blank). I've always felt that a bumper sticker tells the world who you are and what you value, and I've never found one that I'm comfortable displaying on my car.

On a long car ride with my husband recently, I happened to bring this subject up after passing so many cars on the road with bumper stickers. I said, "Honey, if you could put any bumper sticker on your car, what would it be?" He paused for a brief second before he answered with the one thing he is very passionate about—college basketball. So his one word was, "Duke."

I was kind of surprised that he didn't have some sort of a spiritual response because he also has a great passion for the Lord. He then asked me the same question, and all of a sudden it hit me like a sledgehammer. If ever there was a bumper sticker worthy of being stuck to my car, it would be my mission statement. It's what I tell everyone. It's the bottom line in life. My mission statement is simply, "Life doesn't work without Jesus!" I would proudly display that on my bumper if I ever found one.

That bumper sticker is the absolute truth my friends. I've tried life with and without Jesus, and I can testify to the fact that doing life with Jesus is the only way. He is the secret weapon I've enlisted for battling my mental illness, and He can be your weapon too. He is that key I talked about earlier that will unlock your heart, dispel all emptiness and fear, and fill you with peace and hope.

My friend, it is not by accident that you bought this book. You didn't pick it off the shelf. God specifically put in your hands. He knew that you would benefit from it and that your life would be changed by it. I have prayed and asked God to encourage all of you who are suffering in silence to share with someone what you're going through. I pray that this book has been able to help you shed any guilt or shame that you've been carrying around. But, friends, my ultimate prayer for you is that you allow Jesus to be your secret weapon in your battle with mental illness. He will give you all the strength and power you need to overcome and have the victory. Engage the secret weapon, and live the life God intended you to live.

My friends, if you are feeling depressed, please tell someone. Your life is more important than your fear. If you are experiencing any suicidal thoughts and want to talk to someone, please call this *suicide hotline number* at 1-800-273-*Talk*. Be brave. Get help. Choose life!

CPSIA information can be obtained
at www.ICGtesting.com
Printed in the USA
LVHW031925060121
675888LV00014B/401

9 781644 683194